THINGS SEEN

Advance Praise for *Things Seen* by Joseph Stanton

Poet Joseph Stanton puts me in mind of those Chinese court literati of the Ming and Sung dynasties who were not simply scholars, but were also expected to compose and recite poetry and to be connoisseurs and philosophers of art, of all arts. What a range is in these one hundred pages, reflecting interests he has long explored in his work, from the questions of what an artist sees and how a painting or art object means, to the moonlit and irredeemably haunted landscape of Noh drama, to the atmosphere and timeless moments of the game of baseball. And what diverse artists he has accompanied into their works—Gauguin, Gorey, Zeshin—giving his attention and language to what they see and what he sees so that we might see, too. He devotes one whole section to the life and vision of an old favorite, Edward Hopper. "Mostly Grimm"—poems based on well- and lesser-known tales—is well named, because Stanton's often playful reimagining refreshes the classic themes and images. Although Stanton has often written directly about baseball, the poems of the final section "Painting the Corners" are particularly interesting because of their several layers and removes. Here the poet/artist notices how the artist sees as he in turn captures fleeting scenes from the art of baseball. Poet and artist have become inseparable in this collection.

—Sue Cowing, author of *Call Me Drog*

Joseph Stanton is a poet of the visual. He willingly and often joyously assumes the ekphrastic stance, his poems moving seamlessly from an interpretation of Paul Gauguin's powerful *Vision After the Sermon*, in which Jacob grapples with an angel, to a series of poems exploring the alienated world of the twentieth century painter Edward Hopper with its emerging complexities and its journey into the dichotomies of the urban and the rural, the internal and the external. Through the revelatory lens of *Things Seen,* Stanton observes the Noh theater tradition, analyzes the Brothers Grimm, and finalizes the collection with a series of observations about baseball as interpreted by paintings, his focus on America's favorite pastime illustrated with an exciting series of engagements. As eclectic as his varied subject matter may be, the basic theme of these meticulously wrought poems remains the same—vision—the act of creative seeing. In the Noh Variations poem "Aya no Tsumi," he writes, "I have spent my soul/on a glimpse of moon/through bare branches." This richly visual collection turns on Stanton's masterful transliteration of image after image into the essence of its own perceived light.

—Laverne and Carol Frith, editors of *Ekphrasis*

Joseph Stanton's tone knows his own "deft, ungraspable self." The wit in this last line from a poem about Gauguin's *Vision After the Sermon*, washes through *Things Seen* with the humility, intelligence and will to have serious fun with famous art—paintings, Grimm tales, noh plays—treated as living experience.

—Paul Nelson, author of *Burning the Furniture*

Joseph Stanton's *Things Seen* is one of the great books of poetry this year that probably will not get the attention it deserves, though I hope my sheer delight might conspire otherwise. His is a major voice and these poems artifacts of an exquisite musical craftsman possessed of a generosity of vision and a special quality of attention that transforms art into being. As the poem about Paul Gauguin's "Vision After the Sermon" offers us, "a roseate window" in which the story "gleams for all to see; / my struggle to know, my difficult wrestling / with that indefatigable god—/ my deft, ungraspable self." *Things Seen* is divided into five discrete sections—ekphrasis that gives fresh insight into that timeless practice; reinventions of fairy tales that remake the Prince Frog, The Fir Apple, Godfather Death and leave us the Shepherd Boy to calculate the universe; Noh variations that demonstrate why that word is derived from the Japanese word for "skill"; a series on Edward Hopper that intertwines his art and life; and deft poems about paintings about baseball—and yet by the end the sections feel as triumphantly cohesive as the movements in a symphony. "Things Seen" offers us the poet at the height of perception and the skills of conjuration.

—Ravi Shankar, founding editor of *Drunken Boat* and author of *What Else Could It Be*

It's always a pleasure to encounter a Joseph Stanton poem, and over the years I've had an opportunity to experience firsthand his remarkable growth as a writer. *Things Seen* takes us to a new level in that growth, demonstrating that the latitudes and heights of his voice continue to expand. "The drift of the unseen song / is what the evening means," he writes in "Thomas Dewing's *The Hermit Thrush*." Immersing us in the unseen song is the intent of these poems—and to a singular extent, what Stanton has achieved. A rich, rich collection!

—George Wallace, editor of *Poetry Bay* and *The Long Island Quarterly*

THINGS SEEN

Poems by Joseph Stanton

BRICK ROAD
POETRY PRESS

Cover art: Winslow Homer, American, 1836-1910, *The Fog Warning*, 1885 (detail), Oil on canvas, Photograph © 2016 Museum of Fine Arts, Boston

Author photo: Franklin Hayashida

Book design: Keith Badowski

Library of Congress Control Number: 2016934331
ISBN-13: 978-0-9898724-7-8

Published by Brick Road Poetry Press
P. O. Box 751
Columbus, GA 31902-0751
www.brickroadpoetrypress.com

Brick Road logo by Dwight New

For Barbara, Susan, and David

Acknowledgments

The author would like to thank the editors of these publications in which the following poems have appeared, often in different versions: *Abraxas* ("Aya no Tsuzumi, The Damask Drum," "Briar Rose," Izutsu"); *Aethlon* ("Philip Evergood's *The Early Youth of Babe Ruth*," "Jacob Kass' *Picking a Team*," "Robert Gwathmey's *World Series*," "Sidney Goodman's *Tryout*," "Sidney Tillim's *A Dream of Being*,"); *Antioch Review* ("Visiting Almost Every Room in Edward Gorey's *West Wing*"; *Bamboo Ridge* ("Hokusai's *Kajikazawa in the Province of Kai*"); *Chaminade Literary Review* ("Thomas Eakins' *William Rush and His Model*"); *BigCityLit* ("Edward Hopper's *Night Shadows*" and "Edward Hopper's *Morning Sun*"); *Cha* ("A Willow-Pattern Plate"); *Concho River Review* ("Puss in Boots, The Sequel"); *The Cortland Review* (Edward Hopper's *Early Sunday Morning*); *Ekphrasis* ("Arnold Newman's Photo of the Hoppers at Home in Truro," "Edward Hopper's *Hotel by the Railroad*," "Edward Hopper's *Skyline, Near Washington Square*," "Variations on a Theme by Winslow Homer," "Thomas Dewing's *The Hermit Thrush*," "Thomas Dewing's *Lady with a Lute*," "Andrew Wyeth's *Wind from the Sea*"); *Elysian Field's Quarterly* ("Nelson Rosenberg's *Out at Third*"); *The Endicott Studio Journal of the Mythic Arts* ("Briar Rose," "The Juniper Tree," "Shibata Zeshin's *Monkey Posing as a Collector*," "The Three Snake Leaves," "Witch"); *Fowl Feathered Review* ("Little Red Riding Wolf," "The Fisherman and His Wife," "The Brave Little Tailor," "The Seventh Seal"); *High/Coo* ("Takasago"); *Kaimana* ("Paul Gauguin's *Vision After a Sermon*," "Robert Delaunay's *Rainbow*"); *The Long Islander* ("Nelson Rosenberg's *Out at Third*"); *poetrybay* ("The Artist Enters the Scene and Keeps Right on Going," "Edward Hopper's *Night Windows*"); *Poetry East* ("Edward Hopper's *Manhattan Bridge Loop*," "The Waters of Life"); *Ramrod* ("Aya no Tsuzumi, The Damask Drum," "Sumidagawa"); *Ricochet Review* ("The Coming of the Demon," "The Monster Nue"); *Seaweeds and Constructions* ("Kantan"); *Spitball* ("A Still Life with Baseball Cards by Kyle

Polzin," "Marjorie Phillips' *Night Baseball"*); *The Spoon River Poetry Review* ("Baseball," "Hansel Lost"); *13 Miles from Cleveland* ("Edward Hopper's *Nighthawks* as Noir"); *Tribeca Poetry Review* ("Edward Hopper Painting *Girlie Show"*); *Vermont Literary Review* ("Edward Hopper Paints Cape Cod"); *Vice-Versa* ("James Daugherty's *Three Base Hit,*" "Bill Purdom's *Classic Fenway Clout,*" "James Chapin's *Veteran Bush League Catcher,*" "Michael Langenstcin's *Play Ball,*" "Sidney Goodman's *"Tryout"*).

"Puss in Boots, The Sequel" was also published in *Troll's Eye View: A Book of Villainous Tales*, Viking-Penguin, 2009

"Catcher" was also published in *Heart of the Order: Baseball Poems*, Persea Books, 2014

"Shibata Zeshin's *Monkey Posing as a Collector*" was also published in *Collecting Life: Poets on Objects Known and Imagined*, 3: A Taos Press, 2011

"A Willow-Pattern Plate" was also published in Ravi Shankar's *What Else Could It Be: Ekphrastics and Collaborations*, Carolina Wren Press, 2015

Contents

Seeing Things

Tales, Mostly Grimm

Noh Variations

Edward Hopper Painting

Painting the Corners

Seeing Things

The Artist Enters the Scene and
Keeps Right on Walking

It might have been his masterpiece,
but he could not leave it at that.
Striding into a foreground of scattered,
refrozen snow and a bitter cold
that made the background sky above
the horizon crackle blue-white
with grief, he wondered why he had
never realized how easy a journey
it could be,
          but, after years of walking,
he could come no closer to the pale,
distant mountains, where God
and his office staff might be waiting.

Clodion's *Dancing Bacchante with Amour*

It is well to dance with abandon
and with Love says this terra cotta
by Claude Michelle, aka Clodion.

It matters not that Amour is not a
man of his word,
but just one of those putti,

a silly cupidity
drunk on what he
thinks must be operatic song.

The dance of this lovely Bacchante
seems to want to play along,
inebriate and voluptuary.

This lover of Love's too blind to see
that either of her cymbals could be
a gong.

Paul Gauguin's *Vision After the Sermon*

I have ordained myself a cleric
in the right-hand corner of this scene
      to picture what these women
of Brittany, through their ecstasy,
could see. All must bow their heads to pray,
      so I have bowed my head,
but cannot pray, nor know what prayer can
know, though I come here to make my art
      discover that God is God
and that angels are winged and dangerous.
That I have had to shape the women's vision
      for myself makes it no less theirs.
An artist's faith must be an inspiration,
and his inspiration must be a vision
      that goes, faithfully, beyond him.
Thus have I spun into my scheme the dream,
the dreamers, and me—who must try to know
      but has not seen the dream.
What the vision sees are two tiny figures—
a blond, gold-winged angel in royal-blue robes
      and a dark-bearded, dark-robed
Jacob. They are grappling on a field
of absolute carmine. This dream's audience
      curves round two sides of the scene,
starting with me and ending with apple leaves.
Jacob, his angel, and the intimate
      wrestling they make together
are cut off from the nodding worshipers
by the apple tree's diagonal thrust,
      which echoes the angle
of my head's lean; thereby, the priest who wears
my face enforces the boundary between
      the seeing and the seen.
Eliminating the middle ground,
I let the story hover in the glare
      of scarlet earth or scarlet air

and make the image mine to make it theirs.
To make the scene profound enough to dream
	I have learned to believe
in a floating world: my wrestlers are
by Hokusai; my tree, by Hiroshige.
	The truth, as always, must be
re-imagined to be real. There's a moral
here beyond this Sunday's sermon and its
	Biblical theatrics.
This picture is a stained glass full of light,
of hope—my mind's enraptured window,
	passionately colored,
carnal scarlet and ethereal blue,
a roseate window in which my story
	gleams for all to see;
my struggle to know, my difficult wrestling
with that indefatigable god—
	my deft, ungraspable self.

Robert Delaunay's *Rainbow*

This Orpheus plays a tune *parisien*.
A cathedral of sacred heart rises
from a high hill that collects *artistes*
at near dead center of this landscaped view.

"Orphic Cubism" was what Apollinaire called
Delaunay's scenery—a form of art
whose song is almost pure abstraction,
aimed to get a rise from the almost dead,

but well-heeled, stiffs of black and brown salons,
not to mention saloons where Delaunay
and his coterie would hoist a few—
orphic insights arriving glass by glass.

Drunk he was on color and its rainbow
arc, a cage of tones to catch a city in,
bending the bow enough to fit his squared
canvas, hiding in pure delight the point

of Eiffel, the turning wheel of Ferris,
and a lovely Montgolfier balloon
ripening to orange and rising to a sky
abstracted to purely green above the clouds.

Thomas Eakins' *William Rush and His Model*

. . . The best art, they say, is that which conceals art.
—Ovid, *Metamorphosis* ("Pygmalion")

William Rush helped his naked model down
from the pedestal he had placed her on.
She had been for him the Schuylkill River—
all in the interest of allegory
that undergoes here a sea change,
so that Rush and his unclothed employee
must stand hand in hand in paint, paired emblems
of Eakins's honest gaze and honest art
that wants the image more in the eye
than in the heart with everywhere the mind,
the mind, calibrating a kind of soul
as deeply felt absence of sentiment.

For Eakins, Rush was a forefather,
a role model, an exemplar of mild scandal;
Rush at the start of the age, Eakins at the end,
shocked Philadelphians with the terrible news
that clothes can be taken off to reveal bodies.
The joke here is mythic and photographic—
the sculptor handing down a homely woman
as if she were a polished-marble goddess,
a metamorphosis of Ovid's sexy text,
a demonstration that, for Tom Eakins,
received wisdom could be received
by photograph
and must be, Eakins would say, or be lost.

This was the last of Eakins' many tries
to capture Rush and his naked truth.
In all the rest, the sculptor faced us,
while his nude faced him, giving us her back,
revealing the pose that became the statue:
delicate mythic bittern resting on
delicate mythic shoulder. In those

poses, frontal nudity was denied us.
We had to contend—and be content with—
the frumpy irony of Rush's wife
seated, knitting, on a stiff-backed chair
(as if in any Calvinist pallid parlor)
inches away from the luminous flesh
of the slender, lovely poser for pay.

In our version, both the sweet, young ideal
and its needling counterpart are gone.
The woman here is no nymph in the making.
She is just as coarse and common and real
as you or me; likewise the man here
is a bear with no forebear.

The heavy-set Philadelphian
who shows his audience his back and rear,
as he leans to help his statue down
resembles not at all the slim, nervous
woodcarver of all the other scenes.
The artist here is only Eakins,
within the frame as well as without,
self-portrait as portly Pygmalion,
turning away from us and toward his art,
whose truth is its only beauty—which is,
as it turns out, all he needed to know.

Variations on a Theme by Winslow Homer

1. *The Fox Hunt*

A fox—
harried in snow by a gathered hunger
of crows—

echoes Homer's name, cornered on canvas.
Both fox and name

appear as ruddy diagonals
determined to keep on going,
lunging desperately

through the white fear's
spectral brushwork
that the artist's name

and his animal
cannot rise
above.

2. *The Fog Warning*

The fisherman's home
races across
in the distance,
searching,
anxiously,
for him.

It is about to be lost to view
in the horizon's rumor of fog
that may soon be
the only thing
he can see.

3. *The Gulf Stream*

The waiting is
all he has
to hold onto

besides the stalks of sugar cane,
sweet last straws to grasp
in hopes that help might come.

Even now a phantom ship
teases the horizon—
one of the dreams

he'd have to be
unframed to see.

4. *Right and Left*

Two ducks suspended in mid-air
above angry green waves.

One, bullet-struck, dives to its demise;
the other, about to fly away,
will have to live without its mate.

Neither life nor death,
neither right nor left,
the artist tells us,
is entirely without fear.

Thomas Dewing's *Lady with a Lute*

Dewing has a passion for the Lady with the lute.
We cannot avoid
knowing that.

Though her almost classic face lifts to light
in full profile, her torso twists
ever so slightly

to show her décolleté,
her bosom surprisingly exposed
above her slender waist.

Men linger in front of this picture
in its corner of the National Gallery
till their wives pull them past.

As a whole, the picture
seems austere—
a decorous

dark-green dress
against a decorous,
dark-brown background,

but, lest we miss the eros of the curves,
Dewing echoes them exquisitely
placing the lovely swell of the lute

in the lady's delicate, pale hands—
where, we can surmise,
the painter wanted to be.

Thomas Dewing's *The Hermit Thrush*

This painting is all gold and green
with a hillside and trees
and women listening
to the thrush they cannot see.

For Dewing
the drift of the unseen song
is what the evening means.

Andrew Wyeth's *Wind from the Sea*

We barely glimpse a slice of sea,
remnant of what the window
held in view.

Through a café au lait haze
we see broken curtains rise
to the breeze's blow.

Tattered lace lifts
blooms and birds,
sighing what dark trees deny,

while the horizon
whispers last words
and distant crows cry.

Shibata Zeshin's *Monkey Posing as a Collector*

Zeshin has made a monkey out of someone here.

Is it the bourgeois patron of the arts
who sees himself redeemed, saved from his lack
of aristocracy by taste, or something like it,
finding his simian true self captured
in delicate, refined shapes of netsuke?

Or does the artist ape himself, mocking
his own ambitions to be lacquerer supreme,
master of artifacts he makes, collects,
and recollects, as all around him old Edo
is roaring toward becoming Tokyo?

Or does he have us in mind, as we stare
at these wittily bizarre reflections,
the deftly arcane musings of Shibata Zeshin,
whose secrets we pretend to fathom,
aping the pose of refined collection.

The Monsters of Salvador and Maurice

Salvador Dalí's *Inventions of the Monsters*
begs its question: do we invent our monsters
or do our monsters invent us?

Dalí's cruel designs swarm within the tabula sub-rosa
of his mind's open eye,
slashed across when least expected,

so that his just desserts brim with monstrosities,
the anxious fruits
of his desolate garden paranoiac.

But in the kinder dream
of Maurice Sendak,
hulking ogres are no more

than the wildest things
our hearts can voyage for
and passage through.

I want Sendak to be correct, of course,
but I seem to have lost the knack
of my elusive childhood's boat,

adrift as I am in my every day's vast expanse
of melting clocks
and burning giraffes.

Visiting Almost Every Room
in Edward Gorey's *West Wing*

You note the moon,
hanging behind the front cover's line of roof,
is a pale skull
full of not being alive.

As you linger
in the vestibule of the frontispiece
the shadows take away
most of who you are.

The carpet in the first room
is concerned with its own crosshatchings
and could not care less
that you have entered.

A door in the next room
disgorges a woman in an antique, black dress
who inclines to a grief
she cannot explain.

In the adjacent room
two white sneakers lounge together,
whispering before a window,
while a third considers them with longing.

Then one door after another
opens before you
without admitting
anything.

Though a dream landscape opens
a window towards a gorgeous distance,
the gazebo at the end of the road
looks to be a skull.

A mustachioed man in a fur coat
has taken off his hat
and sits uneasily on a chair
leaning on his cane;

when he opens his eyes,
he will be staring
directly at you.

A naked, bearded man,
posed contrapposto
has turned away from you
in front of the balustrade

and does not care to note
that a bronze bust in the next room
precisely echoes
the turn of his head.

White sheets
floating in mid-air
are determined to reach
the ceiling.

The bearded man,
now fully clothed,
lies face down on the floor,
dead.

A calling card,
rests awkwardly on the carpet,
whispering a name.
A ghost peers through a window.

Hokusai's *Kajikazawa in the Province of Kai*

A cormorant fisherman
tightly grips lines balanced

on the tip of a wave-rocked reef,

precarious yet firmly fixed
in the center of swirling sea and sky.

The strings he strains at complete
a triangle more powerful

than the mountain that echoes it
through a distance of blue air.

A Willow-Pattern Plate

The castle looms blue on the porcelain plate.
A boat—blue, too—sails off-shore,
sinister in its whisper of winds,
while the beautiful daughter and her furtive lover
cross the blue bridge in the cool rain
and embrace under the blue willow.

When they look up from their passion
two gigantic birds,
ridiculous in their unlikely warp of wing,
have filled most of the glazed white of the sky
with a verve décoratif.

By the time you have finished
eating the last of the crumbs off the plate
the lovers have achieved their blue consummation,
devoutly, behind the porcelain temple
and sailed off in the blue boat,

while two men—
a wealthy suitor and the girl's father—
watch in azure silence on the pale bridge
as ceramic willow leaves
                    fall and fall.

Tales, Mostly Grimm

The Blue Light

At the bottom of a well
gleams a bright blue light

that might be the means
to rule the world

or just another way to die.

Bearskin

Homeless and starving, a soldier agreed
to wear a bear as if it were his skin
and for seven years to be
servant to a kindly gentleman

he knew to be the Evil One.
Still, a job's a job in good days
or in bad, so he did for seven
years the devil's work, hidden away

from the sun and the smiles of heaven
and the joys of the everyday.
Yet, in the end, this Satan
paid Bearskin his promised pay,

wedding the, now furless, soldier
to the loveliest of wealthy daughters.

The Fir Apple

When murder sought the children,
the boy became a rose tree
and the girl its single bud,
and the witch was deceived.

When murder came again,
the boy became a fir tree
and the girl a fir apple waving in the breeze,
and the witch was deceived.

When murder came yet again
the girl became a pond
and the boy the duck that swims on it,

but the witch was not deceived this time
and tried to drink pond, duck, and all,
so the girl pulled her in and drowned her.

The children returned home happy,
and, if they are not dead,
they are still alive today.

Jorinda and Joringel

Dapper Jorinda and lovely Joringel
wandered so far into the dark wood
that an evil castle loomed above them.

The witch in residence
transmogrified Joringel into a nightingale
and clapped her in a basket,

where Joringel mournfully sang
"jug, jug, jug"—
but there was no poet near to hear.

There was only the witch,
wicked and accumulative,
who carried Joringel

to the castle gallery and added her
to a renowned collection of seven thousand birds
who had all once been beautiful girls.

Meanwhile a dream led grieving Jorinda
to a flower with a jewel
of dew at its heart.

With this magic gem
he opened all enchantments
and, at the last, destroyed the bird-obsessed witch.

All at once, Jorinda, conflicted and confused,
found himself in the midst
of seven thousand featherless and grateful maidens,

and Joringel, too.

The Boy Who Wanted to Learn to Shudder

Despite ominous threats
everywhere at hand—
corpses hanging in air,
demon cats around the fire,
a ghost lurking on the stair,
a giant spirit with a long, white beard—

a brave-enough fool might
fail to find fear forever,
living on and on,
regretfully shudderless,
married, unhappily,
to bliss.

Briar Rose

This is the way the world should be.
Beautiful daughters do not die.
Instead, the universe stops with her breath,

which becomes the timer for everything else,
so that, when a miracle undoes her death,
all of us—every father, every friend,

every fly on the wall, every budding leaf—
awaken to gather round her, to laugh
with joy that she is here and so are we.

The Brave Little Tailor

He killed seven at one stroke
(seven flies on his jam pot)
and so he awoke to the lovely thought
that he must be a mighty hero.
Strange little man that he was,

he harbored no doubts and bragged with pride
of his ridiculously fearsome prowess.
Though all he had on his side
was an oversupply of cleverness,
he defeated a pair of giants,

a terrible boar, a ferocious unicorn,
and several troops of befuddled men.
Of course, in the end, he married a princess,
proving, once again, that a well-played bluff
can knock the stuffing out of brawn.

Clever Elise

One day,
her supple brain
devised the thought

that Elise, her very self,
was already at home
in bed with her husband.

Dissuaded by this ingenious deduction
from knocking on
her own front door,

and fearful that she was not,
in fact, herself,
Elise set off in despair in search of Elise

and was never heard from
again.

Listening to the Crows

The crows who'd like to make a meal of us
think we do not know what shadows sing—
how dew lurking in grass can heal the eyes,
how shifting a stone can loose the waters of life,
how listening with care can make us kings.

But we must not let the darkness see
that we have heard its song
or it will fall upon us with a fury,
cruel beaks jabbing and jabbing,
till everything we've known is gone.

The Fisherman and His Wife

A purity of heart
can be a sea calmed by kindness.
But a greed for home renovation—

the richest carrara for countertops,
the rarest ebony for floors—
can make

the sea grow grim and violent,
the waves marbled with frowns,
the sky lurid

and disapproving.
Oh, wife, dearest one,
let us rest content

with our congoleum,
lest our wishes leave us
roofless.

The Flax

Above the field of flax wave flowers
blue as a sky purpled by a hint of sunset
or a whisper of blood—
their petals delicate as wings of moths.

Each five-petaled cerulean
lasts less than a day, but each plant
makes a score of flowers,
a field blue as far as we can imagine.

Hans Anderson
has the flax sing
the joys of all that happens—

the opening to the sun,
the cloth for concealment,
the relentless wearing down

of the tissue of words,
words that might or might not be wise,
and then the magnificent burning that releases
all we've tried to say.

Prince Frog

To me she was as dear as dear can be,
the endless hours and days I crouched fondly
beneath the bank concealed,
as she played with her silly ball, lovely
she seemed to me who had scant hope—
despite my dreams that I could be a prince
if brought into her bed—but then she dropped
her precious toy, and I hopped to my chance
and ascended to her entwining sheets
where I found myself a man and a king.

Yet beside the bank once again I dream,
recalling the feel of wet skin against wet skin,
as I gaze upon green women I might have known
had I not been a fool for a ball badly thrown.

Godfather Death

A doctor made a deal with Death,
and it might have remained
his ace in the hole,

his means to cures miraculous
and mysterious.

But such contracts are perilous,
to say the least, and he was undone
by the purest of desires,

his candle snuffed
by nothing more than lust.

The Golden Goose

The two clever sons scorned
the homeless man who begged a bite.
Each claimed to be too wise
to share their ample provisions,
but the third son, dunderhead that he was,
pitied the haggard, hungry old man
and offered him all that he had,
his meager ashen cake and sour beer.

As fortune would have it, though,
the geezer was magical:
the cake tasted fine,
and the beer became a delicate wine.
And then—wonder of wonders—
the old man bestowed a goose of gold
to thank the youth for his kindness.

As the foolish son walked down the road
with the golden fowl under his arm,
seven times he was grabbed at
by seeming-wise, self-serving citizens,
and each of them stuck fast,
causing, as they passed beneath the castle,
a dour princess to laugh
for the first time in her life.

The princess soon learned to love
the dunderhead
and married him,
making a sweet idiot
the unexpected king
of everything.

The Goose Girl

They slaughtered Falada,
her much beloved horse,
and nailed his head to a high post,
and she lost her name, her place,
and the much remarked beauty of her face.

And the dead Falada sang,
"Princess, Princess,
if your mother only knew,
her heart would surely
break in two."

And the Princess sang,
"Oh, Falada, hanging there.
Oh, Falada, hanging there."

Of course,
a deus ex machina
happened to be listening

and struck down her glib and clever foe
so, at the end of all,
only for the treacherous
(and, of course, for Falada)
has this been a tale of woe.

Hansel Lost

Gretel, the darkness rides
beside me on all roads,
grim edges serrated by trees.

Dark forests lurk, too,
on all horizons,
portents ahead,

rumors behind.
All my days I pocket
every thought, or try to,

white pebbles stowed
against the night's end,
the dawn's breaking.

I whisper words of comfort
to no one there,
having outlived

all parents, all witches,
all houses of cake,
all sisters brave.

Hans My Hedgehog

A husband loved
might not be as prickly
as he appears.

But, then again,
he might be
worse.

Brandished knives
can end
lives.

Jack and the Beanstalk

We have all known
since childhood
that there ought

to be a way to ascend
to the land that is the sky,
glamorous

with its rolling scapes of clouds,
its castles of dream,
where magical things

might be closeted,
ready to hand
for a clever lad,

murderous and quick
and fruitfully
greedy.

Joys and Sorrows

His claim was
that he shared with his wife
both joys and sorrows.

When he hit her,
he professed to be full of joy,
and she of sorrow,

but, when he missed her,
he said, it was she who had the happiness,
while the sadness was all on his side.

But up and down our street
all we knew of them
were his angrily shouted expletives

and her shrill cries of pain
and the endless, endless weeping
after he had gone.

The Juniper Tree

She so desired a child
the world had to yield it up.
When she bled, by accident,
while cutting an apple
under the juniper tree,
the heart of things opened,
rising through the roots of the tree
and reaching everywhere,

her love sprouting in all the leaves
of every tree, a forest
where all the branches intertwined,
growing together, tangled
and dense with birds singing
and blossoms falling,
as gentle as the clouds of joy
drifting inside her mind.

She devoured
bright, scarlet juniper berries
until her swelling reached
its ripening and her body spoke
its perfect little boy,
as red as blood and white as snow,
and she was so very very happy,
strange to say,

that she could only die,
dreaming herself a tree
of never forgetting,
dreaming her beloved boy a song,
beyond most kinds of dying,
singing the gold's shine,
the red shoe's dancing,
the stone's grind never ending.

The Lady and the Lion

She had hoped someday
her prince would come,
but, as events unfolded,
it was she who had to come to him,
in payment for a rose purloined,
and, though he was an enchanting fellow,
and she loved him with a passion,
it turned out that his enchanting

had made him
a lion by day, a man only by night,
and, when he finally saw the light,
his charms had rendered him
a fly-by-night white dove
roving through the wide world,
a flirtatious ladies' bird,
dropping a white feather here,

a white feather there,
hints of a path
that might give her,
his one and only true love,
a shot at winning him away
from that formidable dragon,
the other woman,
the ultimate femme fatale,
a mantis who'd have eaten him
as soon as look at him.

In this tale, at least,
it is the heroine
who is truly the heroine,
her prince, at best,
whether lion or dove,
an absurdly endless labor of love.

Little Red Riding Wolf

The wolf cub surprised by a sly child
along the woodland path
suspected no bad intent,
despite the rude inquiries
and the cleverly concealed shotgun.

Yet once upon the time
the cub arrived
at her grandma's door
where she dreaded the small teeth and pale hair
lurking behind grandma's fur.

The Princess and the Pea

The extremity of her sensitivity
impressed a richly idle princely family,
who could not see they missed the real pea
of her discomfort, bothered as she had to be

by the absurd softness of the ample beddings,
not to mention the pillow piles aggravating
her much lamented acrophobic dis-ease.
As years passed by, she taught her king

how a board under the mattress aids the spine
and keeps it straight and ready for laughter.
Under her guidance, both wise and refined,
the kingdom prospered, happily ever after.

Puss and Boots, The Sequel

In the aftermath, the cat's out of the bag.
No longer content to be a clever slave

to a clueless master, Puss lands on his feet—
his hostile takeover so smoothly engineered

that his former master barely discerns
his own dismal, sudden passage back to rags

and the cat's ascension to the dream
his cruel intelligence has earned—

the vast estates, the naïve kingdom's crown,
the gorgeous, cat-adoring queen.

The Shepherd Boy Calculates the Universe

Dam all the world's waters so nothing flows,
and I will know how many drops there are.

Give me a sheet of purest white,
and I will fill it with as many lights as there are stars.

Let me watch the bird peck away the mountain,
and I will tell time down to its last loss.

The Shoemaker's Rumpelstiltskin

You fools spy on me from behind your curtain
as I turn over in my hands your ridiculous gifts—
shoddy doll's clothes I could have stitched
better in five seconds,
and with gold thread if I'd liked.

What need I of your pitiful presents?
Better that you get yourselves back up to bed
and make me a child—
that is what I will demand,
what suits my taste, my appetite.

The Spindle, the Shuttle, and the Needle

A work of art can be the story of its making,
every stitch in time a spindle spin
that chases the spinster's

might-be lover—
a prince, of course—
as he rides away from her,

never to return he thinks;
but then the plot thickens
into a woolen-carpeted

semblance of home,
a craftily shuttled welcome,
abetted by a needling

that so embroiders
the prince's return
as to make sure

the maiden's lovely stitchery
weaves an artful spider's web
from which he will not want to escape.

The Star Money

The death of father and mother
left the girl lonely and bereft—
no home beyond the clothes she wore,
no food beyond a bit of bread.

Out she walked far
into the cold and dark.

A poor man cried his hunger
so she gave up her bread.
A child complained of cold ears
so she gave up her hood.

A baby shivered in the rain
so she gave up her socks.
A girl begged covering,
so she gave up her smock.

She stood naked beside the sea
and had not one single thing to show
beyond the greatness of her grief,
the bottomlessness of her sorrow.

Then suddenly the stars began to fall
all around her. The clear cold night
rained coins of silver, coins of gold,
and she was, at last, clothed with light.

Stupid Hans

To win the day
speak honestly.

Say, for instance,
that apples are apples.

Admit that a boat is a boat
and not a wooden spoon,

and you may be the one
who sails your ship

through the squall
of no chance at all.

Three Heads in a Well

If you meet these three—
afloat, grimacing, golden—
take care that you take care.

Gently comb tangled hair
till gold falls free.
Cleanse encrusted ears
till silver fills your hands.
Wipe snotty noses
till they sneeze forth coins.

Whatever you do
these grinning skulls
will not seem to judge.
But beware of spurning the bodiless.
A floating head can hold a grudge.

The Three Snake Leaves

When one of us dies
let the one who lives
travel underground

to steal the three leaves
from the secretest snake
and place them

gently but with haste
at the three doorways
of the cold body:

one for the right eye,
one for the left eye,
one for the mouth.

Both of us must swear to this
or neither of us can
live forever.

The Waters of Life

The mad old man, your father,
is dying, his mind's life
lost in a dark fog.

To save him you must find the waters of life,
seeking advice
of the snarling dwarf,

the murderous troll,
the withered hag,
the indifferent doctor in his white robes.

There will be a long, long ride
through the wilderness of your heart,
and the path will be fraught with monsters.

But you must keep faith
with this night's fearful dream,
remembering

he would have done
the same for you,
and did.

Witch

This forest heavy with dark humor
frames direst need into a candied home,
whispering lies of taffied architecture,
a sweetmeat trap for the lost or abandoned.

An oven is a place to warm the heart
for hags who favor giblets with their meals.
This witch loves to devour every part.
She likes to see to all the small details.

She smiles to show she has no grudge, no gripe.
Her hunger is the only thing she feels.
No malice makes her want to take your life.
Your bones she'll toss upon the apple peels.

Noh Variations

Hanjo

A husk of himself, he waits and waits
for his one and only lover,
lost to him for all his life of loss,

his heart a single leaf fallen
on waters
dark with the dregs of a city

while he dreams himself an azalea blossoming
in the thickening darkness of a wood.

She said she'd return in autumn
but so many autumns have come and gone,

his bed empty first and then his mind,
till he took to living in a shopping cart,
gazing always down the walkway.

In his hands he holds a memory of moon.
In his dreams her hands
seem to be the moon flowers.

Would they know each other now,
if she should happen
to stroll his street—

she brandishing her suit for business,
he rattling his can for coins?

Takasago

An old man and an old woman
tend the lonely pines that stand
at Takasago and Sumiyoshi.

They are gnarled and knowing,
deathless ghosts of each other's heart.

Centuries dead,
they preserve each other's spirit
through careful gardening.

These trees remain green
through endless layers of death;
they bend forward towards
the same expanse.

Izutsu

Under beads of dew in tall grass a cricket cries.
The abandoned daughter
sings her elegant, selfish lover
over treacherous midnight, or tries,
for all the good it does her.

She would cleanse her eyes in moonlight,
but the water rippling in the well
unravels her face until
it is only his.

Aya no Tsuzumi (The Damask Drum)

Here in my dark garden
I pound and pound the drum
that makes no sound.

My love for you
is a white bird
with a flower in its beak
that rises
outside your mind's window
on wings
that beat and beat.

But still you will not hear.
I have spent my soul
on a glimpse of moon
through bare branches.

I will wash my weeping
in shadow
and dream myself a demon
dancing in the dangerous corridors
of your heart.

Koi no Omoni

I could not bear the dead weight of love.

The hopeless hope the lovely lady
asked me to heft, a basket filled with stone,
weighed me down to a bitter death.

There my leaden heart could come to rest,
pathetic as I was, a mere servant in her garden,
collapsed in her chrysanthemums.

In repentance she deigned to kneel beside me,
but I was not moved to forgive and filled her mind
with the molten stone of hell, a heavy thought

from which she could not rise again.
A statue in her own garden she must remain,
a monument to my never ending pain.

Shunkan

All have sailed back to the beautiful things
save only me, who loved them most.
I alone am left here to weather my failings.

I sing the sorrows of a forlorn coast
and hear a plover cry as it flies.

My robes are frayed sand flowers
blooming under desolate skies.
Longing for Kyoto's scented hours,

the wisteria hanging at Hojoji,
the maple leaves drifting down,

I scan a horizon of sea, only sea,
a vast expanse of no thing at all,
a vacancy, an emptiness of sand and sun.

No hope now
for pardon.

Sumidagawa

She has come from a city
more distant than her dreams
in search of her lost son.

Crossing the Sumida River,
she studies the face of the moon
breaking on the water.

The dancing lights
on the approaching shore
create a ceremony.

Prayers for a drowned one
flicker in the cold winds
rising from the deeper currents.

She is destined for the grief
her questions will bring her;
she can see it coming

like the darkness at the end
of an idea.
We in the audience

know this knowledge
will earn her the wrinkled
ogre mask of madness,

and we know she will reach
for the sound of her son's voice
as it dawns from her own mouth,

but the morning
light will swallow
his dancing ghost.

Kantan

You are about to enter
a room with a déjà vu,
after years of wandering.
You are searching for a pillow,
a magical pillow that contains
incandescent images
of the future.
You hesitate at the doorway,
considering the night sky.
Seeing your name in lights,
you expect to star in eternity.

A breeze lifts you into the parlor,
and you stand,
in a half-remembered warmth
talking to an old woman
who could be your mother
but isn't.
Suddenly
the tingle down your spine
chimes midnight,
and you know you are in the right place.

While the gruel cooks,
the pillow comes to meet you
on the matted floor.
Visions fine-tune inventions
of fulfillment.
You sigh at beauty
beyond the stretch of words,
at music played on marble waterfalls,
at flowers that eat their own colors.
You rule the garden with an iron smile.

Torrents of pleasure
tumble you endlessly.

Your smile comes full circle, and,
having rounded yourself into a moon,
you see how your glow ripples the water
and wonder
if you have become
a Buddha.

It had to happen.
Torn from your pocket of joy,
you find yourself
spinning back into the room
where the old woman
hunches before you
asking if you'd like
a bite to eat.

Semimaru

The prince, blind since birth,
discarded on a mountaintop to die
on the brink of adulthood
by the will of the king his father,
rides his abandonment,
a paused flexion of motionless dancing,
a boy-man just barely alive,
tended by a kindly peasant.

Whether in a hovel or a palace,
the prince knows,
no one lives forever.

The sun and moon
have no light for him.
Even the lamp the peasant brings
can be only a flicker of darkness,
but he has his biwa to play,
the first string and the second wildly sound,
autumn wind brushing the pines;
the third string is the rain falling,
driving down on him his misery;
the fourth string, the prince himself
its strum insistent, bitter, almost unheard.

A mad woman,
a princess deranged by the cruelty of a father
and the loss of a brother,
comes wandering,
her hair, disordered and whitened
by the touch of stars and frost.

Because her antics make the peasants laugh
she begins the dance
of pulling hair out by the roots,
a mad cavorting to no tune,

till of a sudden she hears the biwa
of the blind prince and knows
she has happened upon
her long-lost brother,
and there comes
the brief, unexpected, joyous reunion.

Then the mad woman
walks off in madness again,
gone back to wandering,
while the blind boy
keeps on playing, as best he can,
his strings thrumming in minor key,
weeping.

The Coming of the Demon

A crocodile gong
became Yamamba's mouth,
acorns her eyes,
a walnut her nose,
mushrooms her ears,
vines her hair.
The pines of the mountains
oozed sap to make her body.
That's what they say.
That's how it must have been.

A gatehouse abandoned
to the mountain mists
rotted and rotted
until only its thatch remained.
Moss covered that.
Eyes appeared and blinked.
A mouth grimaced and began to howl.
Arms and legs sprang forth,
and she began to dance.
That's what they say.
That's how it must have been.

An old potato
exposed by a slide of mud and rock
spouted white whiskers
that became her wild, wild hair.
The potato became her body,
and, bit by bit,
hands and feet, eyes and ears,
nose and mouth broke out,
and she began to sing.
That's what they say.
That's how it must have been.

An angry old woman seethed
in a village that crouched
under the shadow of a mountain.
The old woman was carried, screaming,
to the highest cliffs and left to die,
but she learned
to eat snow, berries, small animals,
and the occasional priest.
Her hair grew white and wild;
her dancing ecstatic.
That's what they say.
That's how it must have been.

The Monster Nue

Every midnight I rose to the sky
wanting only to kill. Why?
Because I wanted only to kill.

But they came
with their magic arrows
and shot me dead.

They shot me dead
and I fell to my waters,
where now my risings
are only ghostly,

a lucent midnight boatman
that none can look upon,
a monstrous being
that even I cannot bear to see.

I sing now sutras
in a voice the villagers
consider too horrible to hear
and so all have moved away.

Pray for me, priest.
Pray for me night and day.

The sutras say
even a thing without a heart
can become a Buddha.

Edward Hopper Painting

Night Shadows

It is early in the century but late at night.
Hopper has leaned out an upper-floor window.
He is looking down at the sidewalk
and the facade of the business on the corner.
A tall, unseen pole casts a long shadow
that a man is about to walk into.
I want to imagine this man my father,
though that makes me a conception
whose time has not yet come.

In '21 he has not even met my mother.
On this paper street his foreshortened form
is a small gathering of ink,
deposited by intaglio, etched to adhere,
where he strides in a hurry.
Centered on the horizontal,
he is the point of balance
that implies the immensity
of New York City night.

One man walking—solitary, ordinary—
going nowhere in particular,
passing without giving the matter any thought
under the spotlight
of a brilliantly lighted, nondescript corner,
towards shadows
that will keep going
all the way
to the unseen stars.

Early Sunday Morning

Nothing stirs on Seventh Avenue but light
and color, red so red and green so green,
notes that complement the bright
harmony the mind strives to see,
a long-shadowed Manhattan morning,
a subtly melodious 1930
of windows and doors that sing
a broad expanse of street,

but no one seems to be at home here
except the woman painted out in window four,
whose ghosted life returns now as pentimento,
as she suddenly throws open her window,
and cries,
   "Oh, come in, come in my dear.
It's been so long, and we have missed you so!"

Manhattan Bridge Loop

Even though the complex, oddly lovely facades in the background
are bravely facing down the cruel fullness of the slanting light,
it is the horizontal in the middle ground that Hopper wants us to
        witness:
a bridge that could go on and on forever, looping
by the insidious implications of cropping,
while one lone workman,
who is slashed across the shoulders by a swath of light
and who could be the only man alive,
strides purposely towards the edge of the world,
his back mostly towards us,
trying to get off.

Skyline, Near Washington Square

He puts on too brave a facade,
and having lost his companion to fire,
he stands isolate and absurd.

His top story too starkly articulated,
wearing his row of Doric pilasters
like an excess of epaulets,

he stares back at us,
stricken and striking,
across the intervening roof line,

which cuts off,
from our point of view,
his head.

Night Windows

The picture is all about
what the surrounding absence
makes of light
inside where the woman dwells
with her window open for air,
undressed
to her final grace note,
her pink slip.

Naked almost
she knows herself to be
but thinks she has held herself
inside a private moment in 1928,
primping
for what she hopes
her night will bring.

Held tight to her only life,
she's not in the least aware
of what Edward Hopper
manages to see,
riding the evening El,
accompanied by
those crude voyeurs,
you and me.

Automat

The day conveyed a daily round of tasks
from her desk to the next and on and on.

Nothing seemed started, nothing seemed done.
A moment of peace is now all she asks,
as she seats herself by herself, alone
with her thoughts but not lonely—no, not that.

She's full of what her life might be, what
her lover whispered when he saw her home.

For us she is a thing that Hopper made—
a still life, a life stilled—an arrangement
frozen just shy of 1928,
whose respite is, for us, her fate.

Nighthawks as Noir

for Tony Quagliano

It was a scary scene, and I didn't want any part of it.

I could tell that the big man,
sitting alone three seats to my left, down the long café counter,
was casing the joint and up to no good.
He was well dressed, sure,
but too well dressed for this joint at this hour,
sporting a Norfolk jacket
and a natty vest you'd hardly notice because he'd buttoned up so
    tight.
He was clearly not a guy given to small talk.
You could tell he would shoot you as soon as talk to you,
but that bulge in his pocket and the stains on his hands gave the
    game away,
telling me more than I wanted to know about how he made his
    dough.

He was an artist all right,
probably a painter from the look of those colors under his finger
    nails.
That bulge under his coat had to be a fully loaded sketch pad,
a dangerous weapon in the wrong hands.
Every so often he'd yank it out
and scratch away for a few minutes then tuck it back in his pocket.
I could see the couple across from him—
the red-haired dame and her hawk-nosed beau—
were getting nervous and wondering what he was up to.

I figured I'd better get out of there, while I still could.
So I set my glass on the counter and left.
You can see it there still,
if you care to look,
up there on a wall in Chicago.

Edward Hopper Painting Cape Cod

1. *Towards Boston*

His watercolors bear whatever crosses there are,
omitting, almost always, the wires
that might carry our messages—
mine to you,
yours to me.

He bares two crosses here,
enough for two thieves,
but you will find no savior between them,
only a tiny railway station,
vintage 1936,

that once sheltered those
in South Truro
who were on their way
to whatever Boston had to offer
or just come back.

2. *House on Dune Edge*

On the dune's edge
a round turret of a house
is a fitting outpost,
a snug place
to hold a soul inside,
a bastion of sorts
against the harsh winds and seas
of Cape Cod in June 1930.

In a photo
taken in 1984,
we can see that,
somewhere,

behind the new rooms and trees,
the old turret—
if not the dune or its edge—
lingers.

3. *Cold Storage Plant*

These pinks and tans
shape a grim,
jagged mass of warehouse
that has nothing going for it
beyond the way
the open jaw it brandishes
seems bent on swallowing—
the light-blue sky, the dark-blue sea—
purposed as these buildings are
for absolute storage
of cold.

4. *Mouth of the Pamet River—Full Tide*

The sheen on the water sings
the fall of dusk
on a pale yellow house,
an odd nub of habitation
caught between

the road's swerve,
the rail track's delicate diagonal,
the utility pole's crucifixion,
and the interflux
of river and full-tide sea—

all seen in failing, brilliant light.

5. *Ryder's House*

"I can hear the silence,"
one critic said of this intersection
of, seemingly, doorless boxes

that form a dwelling
solid as stone—

offering us no way in,
no way out.

Arnold Newman's Photo
of the Hoppers at Home in Truro

Hopper stares us down
in early morning light,
hunched and implacable.

Awkwardly seated
with his arms winged outward on both sides,
he grips the armrests of the white chair,
as if he were about to propel himself upward,
to rise to his feet
to leave us and Arnold Newman
staring only at his house
whose roof line echoes the spread
(because he hasn't left us yet)
of Hopper's arms.

The huge north-facing window of the house
seems to float above the painter's head
like a cartoon balloon,
waiting to be filled with the grim sunlight
of his thoughts,
while to the side of the house,
outlined against sea and sky,
we can just make out the tiny figure of Jo Hopper
(managing, as she always did, to get into the picture)
gesticulating wildly.

Morning Sun

"A vast and tender / peace / seems to descend / from the heavens . . ."
—from a Paul Verlaine poem Edward Hopper gave
to his wife, Jo

This harsh light seems a kind of voyeur.
She faces it through an open window,
a light that is the gaze of her only Edward
basking on her, his one and only Jo.
With a marriage that seems a kind of war,
how can they stay so devoted, so true?
Attired in the red-orange he'd a passion for,
she's held in his mind's box of green and blue.
He's made her echo the red-brick horizon
that gleams beneath the sky across the street.
Facing the rise of a new day's sun,
she opens to rumors of light and heat,
but the vast, descending peace her lover
has shaped around her seems entirely untender.

Compartment C, Car 293

Compartment C is almost all about green—
the color of the illusory, the fleeting,
the never to be attained,
the sweet spring seasons always out of reach—
a color he usually saves for accents, notes of grace.

Jo here is looking sexy—
in the preliminary drawings it is clearly her—
though the woman in the finished painting,
as so often in Hopper's scenes,
is Jo re-imagined as dream.

Hotel by the Railroad

Though we do not speak, there seems to be a harmony
        here.
The blackened blue of my vest and pants echoes
the blue of the chair in which Jo hunches
reading her dark-blue book. All these things
refer, too, to the somber blues, lightened by ocher,
of the shadows on the wall of our dismal room
and the wall of the windowless building
my gaze cannot avoid considering as I stare
across the burgundy tracks that echo, in turn,
the burgundy of the mirror's frame.
Then there is the forest green in the almost unseen
carpet and the window shade glimpsed around the corner

and the bright yellow, modulated with white,
of the curtains and the hotel's outer walls.
The tracks—which, again, I appear to gaze on,
poised as I am, thinking about all this,
while my cigarette burns almost down to my fingers—
are painted entirely burgundy, for the sake of my scheme,
for the sake, as I have said, of the harmony,
despite the real steel such tracks have always shown me.
These tracks slice past the edge
of where we seem to have stayed the night
in a hotel we will be leaving soon to ride parallel lines,
despite Jo's evident anger, out of this scene and into
        another.

Girlie Show

Puritan by birth, sensualist at heart—
Hopper was struck by something
he wanted to say on Valentine's Day, 1941,
while gazing at a buxom woman,
disrobed and prancing,
on the last stage of the Minsky family's
grand wheel of burlesques
in the old Republic on 42nd Street.

Fed up with Fiorello
and The Little Flower's tedious complaint
against displays of flesh
and wanting to say so in paint,
Eddie asked Jo to pose for him
again and again—
their studio on the top floor
of No. 3 Washington Square North
become a theater runway,
another round in the game they played,
Jo posing, actress that she was,
for another of Eddie's many women.

The first sketch of her in conté crayon
very tenderly rendered
her fifty-year-old body,
nude and lovely,
her arms raised in the stance
of the dancing Girlie,
her legs gaily striding,
her face turned toward the artist,
squinting at him as if to say,

"Is this enough, Eddie,
can I stop now PLEASE,"
shivering but holding her pose,
her firm breast upturned to a degree,
her loveliness especially lovely for him,
as he keeps her in this difficult pose
for his own joy,
and hers, too, if truth be told,
in the intimate Times Square
of their intensely complicated
intersection.

Painting the Corners

Michael Langenstein's *Play Ball*

And God handed Adam
a sphere 2.9 inches in diameter,
weighing just over 5 ounces.
Covered with blanched cowhide
and stitched with red thread,
it contained 369 yards of yarn.
Its heart was cork.

God had taken
seven innings to make it
with attendant bats, fields,
players, fans, vast skies,
a rolling world of earth and ocean,
not to mention creatures and plants innumerable
to surround the stadia.

Then God stood and stretched
and sang "Take me out"
and saw that it was good.
But he would not say how
it would all end.
We'd have to wait
for the fat lady to sing.

Baseball

for the baseball prints of Charles Hobson

1. *Pitcher*

His left leg's a pillar,
a support for the torque of his torso,
warped parallel now
to the gleam of the pitcher's mound.

His left hand
bears a tightly closed glove,
and his right foot,
brandishes a dark shoe.

Born up by the u-shaped silhouette
of leg and arm, his right hand seems
the briefest crest,
a following wave of his body's surge.

Despite his crafty body's
lingering rumor of disdain,
he has, for all we know,
thrown wildly into this grim, oceanic dark—

we find here cheers of light that make for us
the glow of uniform and cap,
a shine that claims the pitch
is singing toward its mark.

2. *Hitter*

His zigzag line of white
capped by a dark helmet,
leans to his pivot,
an action of pure intent.

His swing seeks a fit,
a key to its lock's
one and only click—

a bird's path
splitting through intricate leaves.

3. *Fielder*

The wall the fielder is up against
seems to rise, as he leaps.

His rising will last as long as our watching.
His arms, legs, and cap-beaked head

form a star, followed by a darker star,
a shadow that remembers the sun's vision,

the way it knew what must be grasped
or lost forever.

4. *Runner*

He dreams a leap that seems
almost to get him there,
but home keeps falling away
the faster he runs for it,
his arms pumping, his stride lengthening.

At last the plate seems to arrive,
hovering just one stride away,
but then there are so many varieties of grief
that a chasm opens,
a canyon in the path of the ordinary day,
what's left paused,
afloat above the dark.

5. *Umpire*

He dresses dark
for grim-armed tasks—
a Shiva of sudden gesture.

Final and deadly are
his cruel verticals,
his ecstatic horizontals.

Sidney Goodman's *Tryout*

In the dark ballpark of the baseball dream
you try out naked, waiting with your bat
in hand for the big pitch that never seems
to come and won't because this is not that

kind of tryout. Here a man in shirt, tie,
and black slacks stands immobile at short.
He is your dark dad who wants you to try
and try, as if this were your last resort.

But why do you find yourself trying out
now? You're an adult with a job and debts.
Your life has found its road, its narrowed route.
Baseball and dad are now only regrets.

But still you crouch, bat raised against the dark,
hoping to hit your way out of this park.

Jacob Kass' *Picking a Team* (oil on saw blade)

The choice of me or he or we
is routine, a casual playing out
of a summer evening's last long light,
but for all the years that follow
such small severings can cut deep.
The blade that leaves us in or leaves us out
makes of us something that we will, somehow,
always be.

Those not picked must move away
towards the mothers tending the toddlers,
or towards the facades of the emptied houses,
or towards dangerous ridges that bracket the scene—
saw-teeth below, Manhattan skyline above.

Childhood is seldom simple, though.
In later years the unchosen,
fueled by this little failure,
may far exceed those who are,
in this pre-adolescent twilight,
too readily chosen, too easily loved.

Sidney Tillim's *A Dream of Being*

The blond man, balding and middle-aged,
leans on the white porch rail,
dreaming himself a young boy
walking a blue bike. Behind the blond boy

his best friend, a dark girl dressed in pink,
dances, arms in air, shouting,
round and round the on-deck circle,
while Babe Ruth,

wearing a gray visiting uniform,
has just swung, left-handed and aloof,
and leans away from his strike zone.
His opponents in home whites dot the horizon.

But the man's sisters dominate the porch,
turning away from the action and each other.
No one notices everyone's mother
on her knees tending a plot of flowers

that might be a grave the size of an infant.
She wears a trench coat against
an autumnal chill or an unseen rain.
Her hand clutches her mouth

as if to stifle a scream.
In the distance clouds drift,
plausible and precise in a blue sky
that seems entirely unaware.

James Chapin's *Veteran Bush League Catcher*

His dulled demeanor says that he has seen
it all, has seen every sort of bounce
or soar or bloop a ball, thrown or hit, can do.
He stands huge and blond before us, the hazy-blue
squint of his gaze aiming up and up and away
toward what he knows will soon be beyond seeing.
He fills most of this painted verticality,
his seeming lack of feeling harboring,
the profounder sort of anguish that saints
and martyrs must endure. He knows this ball
will not come down inside the wall,
that this ker-ack! will echo and re-echo
down the evening that has almost begun.

The fans' many faces bend a spectrum
of fanaticisms behind him.
Because he has doffed the catcher's mask,
to put on this show of indifference,
we can painstakingly observe
his impossibly impassive face,
the mask that has become this catcher.

James Daugherty's *Three Base Hit*

Though an artifact of the almost
ancient past of 1914,
this Armory-Show-induced scene
seethes with furious Futurism—
a Boccioni at the bat.
A careening action, this game's
machine has everything and all
at once. The ball is ubiquitous,
but every staring fan is just
a blank wedge of vacated desire.

These intricacies seem to pose
a Rube Goldberg array of gears.
The pitcher winds, fires, and follows
through his motion. The batter misses
two strikes and hits the ball, too,
and his multi-limbed scamper
along the eastern line, is trying,
repeatedly, to get him to first base.

Every fielder crossing our view
receives and throws the many balls,
which are, it seems, all the same ball.
The catcher's bright white and blue
receives the pitcher's pale-hued
and oddly circular contortions,
thrown from left to right and back again.
The pitch here, and catch, is baseball—
its painted joys and their commotions.

Philip Evergood's *The Early Youth of Babe Ruth*

Babe Ruth, in his youth, faced two ways,
the Janus of a time that had much on its mind.
He pitched and hit and the lovely loft
of his swing was a joy forever.
The aesthetic of his play seemed

to crib childhood's secret places—
hills green with delusion, homes
golden with coin of the realm.
Around some corner, a fat man would say,
a prosperity lurks, and Ruth would find it,

again and again, and become a commodity
as much as an icon, his name a bar
of sweetest candy on which he chewed
with all dark delight, his grin
our bright innocence and its evil twin.

A Still Life with Baseball Cards by Kyle Polzin

Lives stilled by Harnett and Peto
sport an abundance of antiques:
newspapers and music sheets,
horseshoes and Faithful Colts,
Meerschaum pipes and violins,
blunderbusses and dead rabbits,
business cards and candles.

Polzin emulates nature morte
for another time:
a baseball nested in an ancient glove,
a bat reclining behind,
an Odalisque of sorts
on a blanket of worn woolen jersey,
all overseen by a catcher's mask
and a shin protector.

But stealing the show
are three cards,
emblems of both
baseball and tobacco.
Though the artist's a Texan,
his three stars of 1909
all ended up in Pittsburgh.

Baseball as lithographic design
could be a kind of Steel City fate
for Howie Camnitz and Rebel Oakes,
ending, as they did,
with the Federals, in cahoots
it seems
with a losing League,

but the third card is the great Honus,
a Dutchman flying in place,
demure against a gold background,

his card worth now three million,
a tad more, one supposes,
than Polzin got
for his painting.

Robert Gwathmey's *World Series*

The sky is as autumnal gold
as the trees glimpsed above the stands
in the cool Wisconsin air.

The World Series winners
rejoice in an exploding cluster
of incandescent home-team uniforms.

The stands are filled with dots
that are the faces of the fans,
many now dead, of 1957.

One of those dots must be the painter
who has dreamed for us
this Milwaukee heaven.

Marjorie Phillips' *Night Baseball*

It's the 1st of September 1951
and Joe Dimaggio
is about to take his last swing
in our nation's capital.
He's up against the great,
but largely forgotten,
Connie Marrero,
El Guajiro de Laberinto,
El Premier of the Cuban stars,
four years older than Joltin' Joe,
but still floating them up there,
one damned knuckle ball after another,
pitching with canny discernment
and elderly grace,
losing game after game,
for the hapless Senators,
despite his stellar ERA.

The electrified white of his home togs
makes him seem a bright X,
marking the spot of green field
that waits under the glowering bruise
of the night sky
suspended above Griffith stadium
in this brief instant before the fateful pitch.

Duncan Phillips has taken his wife
to witness the great Dimaggio,
another masterpiece for their gallery,
but Marjorie can see this night
is all about the weary pitcher,

spread-limbed as if on a cross,
arrayed against the base path
the too much celebrated Joe
will too soon circle.

Oh, where have you gone,
Connie Marrero?

Bill Purdom's *Classic Fenway Clout*

In the foreground, a row of intent faces,
shouting or open-mouthed
in awe or consternation;
hands raised,
fisted or held against the head,
anxiety and jubilation intermixed,
desire and fear conjoined.

Just beyond the fans,
number 19
is waiting on deck,
bat forgotten on his shoulder,
as a tiny speck of white floats in the far distance,
high above the dark-green wall.

The expanse of field is patterned
in lovely swaths of green and yellow-green,
bright under the high, erected lights,
whose spilled milk, blurs to an intensity
that might be God himself
rectangulated and poured
toward this cathedral revelation
that will, however, not end this world
or even this World Series.

The night sky screams black against the white of the lights.
It is as black as the sleeves of the Red Sox players,
as black as the scoreboard that says (for now)

CINN. 6
BOST. 6
and
INNING 12

No stars ride this sky
other than the tiny dot of white,
heading toward the foul pole.
Everything seems to lean toward the disappearing sphere
and toward the batter, number 27,
gesturing with both his arms,
willing the ball to stay right, stay fair.

No one seems to notice the moon,
floating enormous over the scoreboard,
where the clock declares
this moment is, forever,
12:34.

Nelson Rosenberg's *Out at Third*

This fiery image makes the hot corner
seem hotter than the nether regions.
Both ball and runner arrive on fire,
but the ball's hottest, a horizontal burn
across this scene's cornered diagonals.

The stadium, the sky, the impossible
elastic-armed reach of the third baseman,
the down-and-dirty slide of the runner—
all these describe a fierce geometry,
where, though it might have turned out differently,

with a hair's breadth more speed on the runner
or less on the ball, it is now as it will
always be on all sides of these many
triangles that sing here in choral harmony,
"You're out! You're out! You're out!"

About the Author

Joseph Stanton's previous books of poems are *A Field Guide to the Wildlife of Suburban Oʻahu*, *Imaginary Museum: Poems on Art*, *Cardinal Points: Poems on St. Louis Cardinals Baseball*, and *What the Kite Thinks : A Linked Poem* (co-authored with Makoto Ōoka, Wing Tek Lum, and Jean Toyama). His other sorts of books include *Looking for Edward Gorey*, *The Important Books: Children's Picture Books as Art and Literature*, *Stan Musial: A Biography*, and *A Hawaiʻi Anthology*. His poems have appeared in *New Letters*, *Antioch Review*, *Poetry*, *Harvard Review*, *Poetry East*, *Cortland Review*, *New York Quarterly*, and many other magazines. He has collaborated on many occasions with artists, musicians, and other writers. He has received many awards for his work including the Tony Quagliano International Poetry Award, the Cades Award for Literature, and the Ekphrasis Prize. *Things Seen* was a finalist for the Brick Road Poetry Prize. In his day job, he is an art historian and a literary historian. He is a Professor of Art History and American Studies at the University of Hawaiʻi at Mānoa.

BRICK ROAD
POETRY PRESS

Our Mission

The mission of Brick Road Poetry Press is to publish and promote poetry that entertains, amuses, edifies, and surprises a wide audience of appreciative readers. We are not qualified to judge who deserves to be published, so we concentrate on publishing what we enjoy. Our preference is for poetry geared toward dramatizing the human experience in language rich with sensory image and metaphor, recognizing that poetry can be, at one and the same time, both familiar as the perspiration of daily labor and as outrageous as a carnival sideshow.

POETRY PRESS

Also Available from Brick Road Poetry Press

www.brickroadpoetrypress.com

Water-Rites by Ann E. Michael

Bad Behavior by Michael Steffen

Tracing the Lines by Susanna Lang

Rising to the Rim by Carol Tyx

Treading Water with God by Veronica Badowski

Rich Man's Son by Ron Self

Just Drive by Robert Cooperman

The Alp at the End of My Street by Gary Leising

The Word in Edgewise by Sean M. Conrey

Household Inventory by Connie Jordan Green

Practice by Richard M. Berlin

Battle Sleep by Shannon Tate Jonas

Also Available from Brick Road Poetry Press

www.brickroadpoetrypress.com

Dancing on the Rim by Clela Reed

Possible Crocodiles by Barry Marks

Pain Diary by Joseph D. Reich

Otherness by M. Ayodele Heath

Drunken Robins by David Oates

Damnatio Memoriae by Michael Meyerhofer

Lotus Buffet by Rupert Fike

The Melancholy MBA by Richard Donnelly

Two-Star General by Grey Held

Chosen by Toni Thomas

Etch and Blur by Jamie Thomas

BRICK ROAD

POETRY PRESS

About the Prize

The Brick Road Poetry Prize, established in 2010, is awarded annually for the best book-length poetry manuscript. Entries are accepted August 1st through November 1st. The winner receives $1000 and publication. For details on our preferences and the complete submission guidelines, please visit our website at www.brickroadpoetrypress.com.

Printed in Great Britain
by Amazon

24489298R00081